Vanishing Into Life

Vanishing Into Life

A Collection of Poetry

by

Jill Lapin-Zell

ISBN-13: 978-0692484289
ISBN-10: 0692484280

Published by Water Forest Press
PO Box 295, Stormville, NY 12582
WaterForestPress.com

Layout & Design by V.R. Valentine
Edited by P. Valentine

Cover Art © Johan63 I Dreamstime.com

To my children.

Who make me proud and amaze me every day

Acknowledgements

This book would not have been possible without the inspiration, encouragement, support and guidance of my dear friend and wonderful poet, jacob erin-cilberto. He has helped me find my voice. I owe him so much more than I could repay.

I would also like to acknowledge and thank three other gifted writers and good friends who have helped me in so many ways. Dick Reynolds, Lynda Bullerwell and Stacy Miller have each had unique influences on me as I have embarked on this journey as an author.

To all of you, I am eternally grateful.

And then my soul said, "Oh, there you are.
I've been looking for you."

Poetry in this Collection

Poetry in this Collection

A Fundamental Question

the afternoon's turned cool and gray
with cloud shadows and spring breezes
oozing over the mountains
like sweet honey from an over-filled jar
and I'm wondering
why we aren't curled up with each other
on a sofa
legs entwined and heads together
like children whispering outlandish secrets
giggling the remaining day into night

I want to reach out and touch you
breathe in the scent of your hair
feel the rhythm of your heartbeat
as my lips rest against your temple

these aching moments of missing you
eat away at body, mind and spirit
give rise to the fundamental question:
can you come over to play tonight?

Too Much Room

i am younger than really old houses
with decrepit shutters shutting out the winds
of romance—

a mansion of youth

with so many unopened doors

i need you to be the key

unlock me.

no one's really lived here for a
very long time.

Wastelands

My grief cracks
Like driftwood which has washed ashore
An ice-choked river in the depths of winter
Unconceived, I search elsewhere to be born
My body trembles
Dry wood bent beneath prodigious weight
Which must be eased, or else break

A New Number

I don't really
feel any different
than I did yesterday
just the soft whisper
of a calendar page
turning in the night
assigning a strange new number
a new hat to wear
a different perspective
giving pause for thought
and reason to wonder
gratitude for surviving
big, brash and brazen choices
quickened by tender years

and eyes that chose to peek
around shifting corners
into sometimes blinding light
and often pitch black voids
always electing the option
of bright and passionate journeys
leading to an examined life
and a series of mindful lefts and rights
that have placed me on this rock
like so many times before
looking into the open maw
of the continental divide
and musing over the fact
that I don't really feel any different
than I did yesterday

All Sales Final

skin on skin
lies on lies
you once loved me
or did you?
was I just a pillow
for your greedy head?

I was too wrapped up in the illusion
to see that inside the gift
another box waited to be opened

go peddle your wares somewhere else
shower another with your deceit
I no longer accept returns
without a receipt

Vanishing Into Life

Wondering at the mystery
And finding ourselves enthralled
Delving beneath the surface
For the chance to learn a secret
Choosing the path of intention
With integrity and purpose
Remaining honest with ourselves
And opting for true living, always
Honoring the path of knowing
With focused thought and effort
Seeking out profound wisdom
In the innocence of children
Staying present in the moment
And opening the doors of perception
Reaching out with intimacy
And inviting another into your heart
Leaving a footprint in someone's life
And loving for the sheer joy of it
Creating the delicate balance
And taking your place in the one seat
Seeing wonder in everyday things
And delighting in what you have
Doing all this with awareness
And dancing to your own tune
Makes the journey worth the ride

All That Remains

Your hands like ice
Yet I felt their warmth
Your face ghostly white
Yet I saw its golden glow
Few words spoken
Yet our hearts spoke volumes

I'm left with thoughts of happier times
Of evenings filled with endless laughter
When we felt invincible
Before the ravages of a horrible disease
Came knocking at your door
And its relentless grasp
Pulled you from me forever

Remembering

Remembering how our smiles touch
And make our souls dance with each other
Remembering how we can laugh until our sides ache
At nothing at all
Remembering how my breath quickens
When I catch you staring at me
Remembering when I am thinking of you
And you call me at that instant
Remembering the hugs
That I wish would never end
Remembering the sweet warmth of your kiss
Whenever I miss you
Remembering how you wipe away my tears
With the soft touch of your fingertips
Remembering is all I'll have left
When you are no longer here

Lasting Impressions

You made an impression
With your shining smile
And incandescent eyes
Your simple equanimity
And strong, broad shoulders

You made an impression
With rampant curiosity
In the funkiest of places
Full tilt boogie attitude
And your arm around my waist

You made an impression
With a sweet warm kiss
And hugs from way down deep
Studded jean jacket
And beat up old cowboy boots

You made an impression
On a windy Philadelphia street corner
In a Dunkin Donuts at 4 a.m.
With cups of warm steamy love
And lingering gazes

You made an impression
Sweet memories in place
Left a wisp of future dreams
Yet to be realized

Touched

elegant fingers beckoning
reaching and grasping at the ghosts within
caressing the emptiness inside
violated once upon a time
but once was more than enough
to drain the soul
of passion's lifeblood
forever

Feeling My Wings

When passion only brings muted ecstasy
And your powerless strength no longer fortifies me
I'll shed the blanket of you that once warmed me
Why should I settle into your nest of twigs
Only to be fed your worms of wisdom?
I'd rather feast on love and
flourish in the garden of someone else's delight
Leaving submission to take flight
And welcome the harbinger of my freedom

Anyone Can Be A Lover

More than anything
Show up in every moment
Be faithful to the ties that bind
Give and receive with no agenda
Fly high and free without a net
Have total faith in someone else
When it feels terrifying
Be emotionally available
All you need is to risk

Anyone can be a lover
Overcome the shadow of fear
In the naked truth of who you are
Invite another to witness
The light shine in and out
To keep you safe
Pull down the old stone walls
While the winds of vulnerability blow
Stand straight and tall
All you need is to trust

Anyone can be a lover
The memories that haunt
The joy that slipped away
The times you wound up hurt
Trauma carried from childhood
Wounds almost healed
To your deepest longings
Allow a beloved access
The courage to open it

All you need is a heart
Anyone can be a lover

Attitude Adjustments

I've written my way
out of writer's block
in the past
fellow poets
prodding me
to keep pen on paper
for ten solid minutes
spewing all I know
about mashed potatoes
or games chalked
on the macadam
of my youth
or my memories of the counterculture
and moments later
write for ten minutes more
about my past lovers
and then everything
I remember about
my grandmother's hands
my funk dissipates by discipline
the hours fly by
measuring words
fine tuning images
and dancing to the rhythms
of lyrical symmetry

Thirsting For You

Slip into my slumbering soul
Breeze into my breathless body
I'll drink you in and
feast on you forever more

But alas

Incessant isolation
Lingering loneliness
Relentlessly remain
Once I realize
You're otherwise occupied

Bittersweet

styrofoam heart

dark roast dreams

filled to the brim

emotions brewing

sweetened by your kiss

and lightened by your voice

let me savor you

until there's nothing left

but the ground

Tailored Touch

Rip my stitches out
Pull with all your might

I won't be mended
I won't be altered
I won't be tailored
To suit your needs

I'm a custom-made garment
So toss aside my mannequin heart
And measure out your love
So that it's a perfect fit for me

Carving Lessons

cruel chisel
chipping away at my heart of stone
marble dust floats to the floor
as you break off pieces
of my alabaster reserve

Droned To Death

incessantly trudging
wordlessly enduring
tearless cries of mechanized man

once upon this manufactured life
somewhere back in time
we sparkled with verve
took drinks from enthusiasm's waters and
ate from animation's plate
while we grew our spirit in gumption's forest

stolen moments from those times
are all that remain
just long enough to remind us
that passion is not produced on an assembly line
and love does not march in automation's parade

Suspended Animation

pages of words strung together
no story told here
she will compose her own
because she has
put her life on hold
keep that thought that it will get better
but
it does not.
no worse
but no better
wait 40 years to follow your heart?
bad idea....

or maybe not
will it be sweeter if you do?
therein lies the irony...
one never knows

sweet pain
happy torture
miserable joy
she knows them all intimately

she suffered and she waited
she cried and she hurt
she lived and nearly died
inside and out
first love
second chance
third draft.... of her life
which has been spent living
in another person's prison.

Surf's Up

try to flood my battened-down heart with your fury
and I will respond with gales of laughter
you cannot categorize me
or predict what I will do
when you surge into my life
with your eye on the prize

I won't be taken
I won't relent
I'll stand my ground
with firm intent

beat on my door
and whip me about
but I'll see tomorrow's light
as I usher you out.

Exit Strategy

like Aphrodite rising from the foam of the sea
you rise from the mist of my thoughts
to become my muse and lead me
away from the harsh realities of this earthly existence

with each excursion we travel a little further
deeper into the realm of obscurity
only to return each time
but how I long for that ultimate trip...
the one that allows me to remain with you

waves of desire wash over me
lulling me into submission
calling me forth
carrying me away

and then
just like that
I'm back again
marking time
and
awaiting your inevitable return

Stock-up Sale

check out my heart
peruse my dairy case
roam my aisles
scan the price of my love
no more canned goods
I'll spice up your life with
condiment wishes
and saucy dreams
love is perishable
so just don't cross me off your list
before the store closes

Fired Up

It's more than being in love with you.
It's more than dreaming of being with you.
It's even more than passion.
There is a fire between us
That will not be drowned by even the hardest rain
A fire that burns eternal
And grows hotter
With each encounter
It began as a spark
So many years ago
And now it is a conflagration
The likes of which I never imagined possible

Blazing tears
Stain my face

Sweep the ashes away

Spring Redux

let my grief mulch the gnarled roots
from which it grew
and make a whiter blossom
which will forge a bloodier berry
for the sparrow and the jay

Forever Elusive

Crystalline dreams
From shattered moments
Pearl dust slipping through my open fingers
Like sands through a sieve...

Wisps of wishes
In voracious emptiness
Haunt my waking hours
Until the merciful night comes
Providing temporary respite
From this stark reality that torments my soul

Shooting Blanks

you've gone AWOL
recalcitrant soldier
leaving me at the mercy of enemy lines
that threaten to ambush me
and make me their POW
I'd much rather be writing the battle plan myself
so that you could instead have your
purple heart
and your honorary discharge

Goodbye Warmth

The warmth of my tears
Mingles with the warmth of our kisses
But that combined warmth
Will never even come close
To keeping me warm till we meet again.

Drink me in
Soak me up
So that I might stay inside your heart
Forever

Second Coming

The moon's eye across my back wakes me
She sighs, "It's time"
For so long I've slept on the floor
A penitent, curled in a sleeping bag cocoon.
But tonight, Lazarus-like, I rise and
Stumble towards the elusive light
Beneath the rain of hawthorn petals
The rivulets murmur
Eddies toward the willow, where I see you
Your fingers probing the stream's depths
So many years, and still I seek you
I've loved no one since you
I call your name but the person who rises
To contest my coming is someone
I've never seen before

Instant

Walls shed clocks and pictures
Like trees disrobing

Imperfect nail heads extend
Like darkened moles

Outside, workmen clothe the house
In aluminum

I am a baked potato

The siren kettle calls
Add water
Crystals become coffee

Groovin' Bones

Sitting in an open field
Ears eager to hear
Hands ready to clap
Legs longing to dance
As the wind blows warm
And fragrant, exciting
Open minds and hearts
And tickling cherished memories
Oh how we love it
This gathering under the sky
Friends and strangers
Freaks and straights
Ready for the music
To light that fire

In souls primed to soar
And ride the magic
As the first chords
Ring out loud and true
The people rise as one
Bones old and young begin to groove
Each to its own personal boogie
Faces starting to glow
With rhythmic smiles and giggles
Same as it ever was
And note by note
Chord by chord
Lick by lick
The magic comes calling again
Lifting our spirits

Keepsakes

Stolen moments
Lingering looks
Feathery kisses
Warm fingers holding on

The aura around us is like a haze
That temporarily separates us
And protects us
From the rest of realty beyond it

I remain within that barrier's walls
As long as I am with you
Because what lies on the other side
Is my world without you

Our song needs another verse
Our story needs an epilogue
For I will move on
Yet
At the same time
I won't

You will always have me
And in my heart
Part of you
Will always be mine

Passion's Grave

My shattered emotions rest in pieces
Gone too soon
To know the rapture
That could have been
Should have been

Once upon a yesteryear
My heart was ripe for the taking
It beckoned you
It beseeched you
And then it died a slow death
When your heart turned away

Now the darkness approaches
Too late to resuscitate
No chance to reincarnate
Can only now emaciate

Lost Kingdom

wanton wishes
lascivious looks
once desired and welcomed
now a distant, hazy recollection
no longer on passion's horizon
mystical mirage
dried up like brittle bones
fractured feelings
and insistent images
torment me
tease me
test me
until
the music rescues me
and takes me away from it all

at least for now

Overdrawn

Miniscule drops of salty pain

teetering on the edge of my eyelids

threatening to fall

ledger of wounds tucked

in the shadowed compartments of my psyche

labeled "never again"

until the next audit

no matter how I try to balance the books

my heart is always in the red.

Meter Reader

Check my meter
Measure out my allowances
In the event that I've incurred overages
Then I'll have to pay up

My valves are leaky
My pipes are shot
Once you come to make those repairs
I'll be good until the next scheduled reading

Only Visiting

We are only here for a brief stay
Where we've been before and where we'll be after this
Are unknowns
So why do we play these games?
Why do we waste precious time apart?
Why are we so complacent to live unhappily?
Why are we so afraid to take risks?
We'll never have a second chance....
Let's live for the moment and grab all we can
Otherwise
That moment will become as unknown to us
As the void from which we came

Necessities of the Heart

Boundless beckoning
Soul's arms reaching into the abyss
Grasping at nothing

Love surrounds me
But never touches me
So near yet so far
Silent voices
Fall upon stagnant breezes
Crippled by atrophy

Spirit slowly sucked dry
Withered hopes dissipate into the void
My grassless lawn, once lush with life
Now fallow and forgotten

Grenade heart
Pull the pin
End the pain
And detonate the dream

On The Menu

gnawing hunger leads me to your table
where I hope to find delectable treats
served fresh daily
so I'll place my order
but your take-out offerings
are all I can get
because I've arrived too late
to have a sit-down repast
couldn't even get service with a smile
so here's my tip...
I'll probably dine elsewhere
and find a corner booth
that allows me to sit side-by-side
with my short-order dreams

The Reckoning

There are times when we reckon
That we know
Who we are
Where we are
And where we are headed.

That is,
Until someone comes along
And breaks down our prior knowledge
Removing our safety nets
Wrecking that to which we used to hold fast

And so it comes to pass
That we need to pick up the pieces
And reconcile our past with our present

Minor Chords

My life used to be
a blues song
twelve bar wails
bent easily
from the pentatonic scale
with brilliant turnarounds
that let in momentary shards of sunlight
to salve my soul
and get me ready
for the next chorus

but oh how quickly
these bluesy minor chords
morph into dancing major ones
stacked one upon the next

when you show up with piercing liquid eyes
these bluesy minor chords
morph over to dancing major ones
stacked one upon the next

Reality Check

Reality smacks us
upside the head and
we see our reflection in the eyes of another
running through life
totally believing that
we're honest in our intentions
lofty and compassionate
in our choices and deeds
when we're really looking
to click through the turnstile
without paying for a token or
giving loved ones their due
then one day someone
who really loves our soul
grabs us by the ego and shakes
the smug pseudo spiritual garbage
from our arteries with a harsh word

an act of powerful kindness that
hurts more than walking on broken glass
rips a hole in the veneer of
intellectual awareness and forces a
deeper look inside to see
truth and how we've been deflecting,
avoiding and covering its razor edge
so our cheek stings from the
smack and the raw look
in the mirror and
if we're lucky, willing and wise we get to
make another choice based on clarity
no longer able to afford the
Teflon-coated self that hides
naked, unmasked and vulnerable
behind the curtain, like Oz

Ancient Union

I called for you across the canyons of time
reached out my hand in open invitation
asking that you join me once again
to explore the magic of our souls' journey home

I would climb and fall 10,000 times
before hearing the distant whisper
that told me you were near
sailing on cosmic winds
toward our rendezvous

I sat beneath the shady trees of my life
learning the virtue of patience
and softly singing the melody of time
so you might find me and begin anew
and there you were with sunbeam smiles
passions that fanned the embers
of countless heart fires lit long ago
in faraway places with mystical names

we come together now with open hearts
sharing a joy born of new awareness
to savor the double helix of life's mysteries
and awaken to the promise of ancient union

Making Room

There is an old circus illusion
clown after clown
jumping from a Volkswagen
defying the laws of physics
and I think
at times that the heart is much the same
jam packed with our own face-painted clowns
fall in love and your heart overflows
have children and more room appears
as they will fill your heart to the brim again
no room for anything else
have a grandchild
and still more room appears
but wait, there couldn't possibly
be space enough for more
but when he's born
bald and new
it's as though
in a suspended instant
another clown
just popped out

Color Me Gray

so many shades of gray
peering through
the pewter colored
screen on my window

nature's wrath
fiercely insistent
angrily unrelenting

cumulous clouds fashion
gun metal dark
at their center
almost blue at edges
that fade into white

charcoal mist hangs
over swaying treetops
and cirrus streaks of pearl
layer upon hoary layer
of slate broken by
patches of light
sleek and leaden

rain falls in torrents
of steel pellets
pounding on defensive roofs
painting my mood
from a palette of mostly
black and white

Worlds Within A World

Asleep on the subway steps
With her tattered heart
And broken spirit
Token dish with a few carelessly tossed offerings
Who were you in the other world
Before you crashed and burned in this one?

Old man
Remnants of your hippie past
To which you cling so desperately
Tie-dyed dreams
Love bead longings
No longer relevant for anyone
But you

Funky chick
Plugged into your music
While the rest of the city
Hurries by
But you don't care
It's all about your own beat

Conference call chic
Couture concerns
With boardroom blues
Can you pencil in a moment from your
Agenda-filled life
Long enough to notice anyone else?

Honky tonk cowboy
With a guitar on your back
The concrete jungle
Seems a long way
From your home-on-the-range life

Ivy league wishes
With elitist strides
Textbook case
Of dissertation dilemma
And classroom confusion

They are us
And we are them
Each of us living in our own worlds
While trying to get by in this one

In the Heart's Time

I can't seem to wrap
My mind around aging
With its homage to aching joints
And knees that hurt like hell
When the rains come
Friends are falling ill
And the end game is creeping up
Like a silent shadow
On a midnight mission
Yet in my heart
Time moves much more slowly
Than seasons pass
But sunsets seem more urgent
Now that they will be fewer in number
And precious music lifts my spirit
Even higher than ever before
I love more freely now

Unafraid of being vulnerable
To men and women alike
As they journey through my life
Planting memories in my mind
And leaving footprints on my soul
Before moving on to perform
The same miraculous gifting
For the next fortunate soul
So, I choose the heart's time
As I sit and grow older
Watching shards of sunlight gently caress
The broad-leafed trees of summer
Knowing that when the time does come
I will embrace its arrival
Because I will have known
That ultimate joy that is love.

Beach Walk

moonlight painting
shiny silver beaches
shadow footprints speak our path
as we walk along the shore
arms around each other,
heads close together
laughing with the wind
telling secrets about the stars
and naming the waves
as they break gently on the sand
barefoot tidal mambo
surf lapping at our toes
sand sliding back to the sea
grain after grain, magically drawn
like a lover going home
and we stop to honor the journey
holding our intention to be as strong
and our love as vital
and rhythmic as the tide

Body Language

connected at the core
riding wave after wave
in a timeless ocean
we fall breathless
sucking at the universe
for precious air
while hearts pound explosively
and hands are left to speak
where there is no resonant voice
to be heard
and nothing left to do
but smile

Dragons in the Void

how many times in youth
did I gaze into the void
and see my reflection
staring back at me
wide-eyed and overwhelmed
by dragons of my own design

each time I took a deep breath
and dove in keeping the faith
trusting that I would only burn
and be consumed if it were best for me

so many times huge fiery exhales
singed my flesh with painful lessons
repeated until learned to the core
and each time I healed and grew new skin
more luminous than the last
and without the need
to be torched so fiercely

until on a cold winter night
I was summoned to the edge once again
and my reflection stared back
smiling and happy to see me

it was then that I knew you were out there
looking into your void
brave and alone
facing dragons of your own design

Boxes

I wonder how many boxes
it would take
to gently store away
the bittersweet memories
of our time together
each in its own snug, hurt-proof compartment
and they would never again consume my days and nights

you've learned to do
that trick amazingly well
box away the secret life we share
that otherwise would take
harsh accountability and
explanation but instead
just call it the past and
it no longer seems to matter

no longer carries the
weight of live emotions and
no one can demand that
you stand and deliver

Oh that you say
done and boxed

it was wonderful
but that was then
and this is now
just move on
there are moments when
I wish it were my way
to fill those boxes with what matters
and stuff them into
some internal storage unit
locking doors to memories
which haunt me and
force me to feel raw

I guess that's why there's
both chocolate and vanilla
choices to make
neither right nor wrong
yet uniquely mine
and so I'll not collect boxes
to store away my memories
snug in hurt-proof compartments
where they will never
impact my days and nights
and in the end
I will heal without regret

Lovers

did you know that lovers
make the mountains rise up
sift the sands that form the desert
fill the seas with deep blue waters
and wring tears from stormy clouds?

did you know that lovers
grow the vibrant sunsets
create the silence in sacred moments
make the ghosts of time laugh
and say which way the wind blows?

did you know that lovers
glow with shimmering light
weave the fabric of cosmic dreams
paint rainbows across the skies
and illuminate the night with star shine?

did you know that lovers are magic?

Contentment at the Threshold

Have you ever wondered
what it would be like
to have the universe serve up life
in the image that you've dreamed it?

Wouldn't it be a kick to find magic
in the middle of a well-fought life?

To answer the doorbell when it rings
only to find contentment at the threshold?

What would be wonderful, it seems,
would be to know I've earned it and
to meet you with a clean slate
filled with experiences but void of baggage

We could meet as equals, willing to try to
put up our hearts as collateral for the journey,
look into each other's eyes for the truth
and find out what it feels like to be fulfilled

Awe

And later
lying in the charged moments
after loving
an embryonic smile
makes its way from
the curve of your lips
and in that instant
of soft drifting union
I look into the face
of a child grown to be
all that is a man

You and Spring

the sun will rise once more tomorrow
slowly nibbling at the cold night sky
until red and orange flames consume it for breakfast
like an egg over easy

the vernal equinox will herald
the arrival of a brand new spring
it is a time of renewal
and the moment to plant the seeds
of a fertile and abundant future

you stand in the middle of those glorious
tomorrows radiant and alive
your smile fueling my days as never before
and gypsy passion painting my nights
with broad strokes of conscious loving
that ignite my soul and call forth the
magic that is our coming together

Whim and Fancy

I think it was your smile
That lit my heart
And made my insides vibrate
With anticipation and delight

Or it could have been
The way you like to be kissed
In quiet moments of surprise
Caught off guard
Standing at the stove
And let me run my hands
All over you, free to touch
Your face, neck and arms
At my whim and fancy
And wrap around you

Until the curve of our bodies
Melds into one another
Blurring the edges of
You and me into we

Maybe it was how beautiful
You are fresh from sleep
Stretching cat-like in bed
Curling into me
For comfort and warmth
Greeting the new day with
Hope and loving tenderness

It might have been any one
Of your myriad wonders
But yes...I think it was your smile

Coming Home

children of the wilderness
find their way home
with a focused turn
of the inner compass

moving to primordial music
droning chants
bone deep
vibrating through my body
bringing it to a point
of sharp focus
honoring what came before
always aware
of how all things change

seasons shift unaided
advancing without hesitation

and I've returned
recently reawakened
to my ancestral lineage
as a nomad
on the path
to evermore

Decoys

I watched a playful pup
have the time of his young life as a
village of prairie dogs played him for a fool

He rushed from mound to mound
only to be distracted by the yips of
another taunting pup
far enough away to be safe
and close enough to tempt

I wondered in my own youth
how often I had run toward
the call of a chimera
only to find myself alone
with an armful of wind

From the vantage of years
and lessons learned
I laughed
at the chase
re-chose the stillness
and the haunting minor chord
that is you

Changes

Each time life takes a sudden turn,
veering north or south, left or right
lifting me up only to set me down
in some new and different place
I feel the child I was so long ago
holding her breath in anticipation
of that very first roller coaster drop

It no longer scares me anymore to change
I just ride the towering waves of discovery
shift direction in mid sentence or
explore the virgin trails that
unfold blazing new vistas at every turn

So when I awoke that day
to find that the destiny had left you
patiently waiting on my doorstep
with your bright and shining smile and
eyes that laughed at the dark of night
I opened the rusty door to my heart and
invited you to dance through my dreams

How was I to know that you were
the lost chord in my life's symphony
a magical sprite that would kindle my flame
and turn my journey into a victory celebration

Now I thank all faces of the great mysteries
for allowing me the gift of your presence
giving me the courage to choose life yet again
and blessing me with your love

Whaddaya Know?

I know more now
Than I did then
More about showing up
Leading with my heart
More about the value of time
And not sweating the small stuff
And living in the moment
You know more too
More than you did then
More about courage
How fear can paralyze
More about choosing to listen
And the gift of space
We both know more now

More than we knew then
More about being comfortable
In our own skins
Taking things as they come
I know more about receiving
You know more about giving
We both can laugh out loud
At our shadows walking
Their backpacks stuffed with choices
Let's meet at the crossroads
With open hearts
The only time is now
Because the past is gone
And the future is an unknown

You're Not Me

I don't love you because
you're just like me
you're not just like me
and I love that

I don't love you because
I think you're perfect
you're not perfect at all
and I love that

I don't love you because
you're so very easy
you're not so very easy
and I love that

I love you because
of the way you look at me
and how you make my breath quicken
and how you are every inch a man

I love you because
you never let me be less
your smile makes me melt
and there is magic in our being

I love you because
we play and laugh like children
you are my special gift
and I love that

In Search of a Rheostat

I shined my light too brightly
A laser beam I'm told
And burned a hole in my beloved
Who left me standing in the cold

The fears he carried with him
From past mistakes he'd made
Provoked his need to finish us
And forced his love to fade

So now he feels much safer
Not vulnerable or exposed
And I sit here in sadness
As doors have all been closed

I'll try to cull the lessons
Find dimmers for that light
But that won't change my missing him
And it sure won't make things right

They say when hearts get broken
Your hopes and dreams must go
But I will always think of him
When the winds of sadness blow

Long ago, a dear friend once asked me to define what it felt like to be in love. It seemed like a simple question, but the more I thought about it, the more difficult it seemed to nail down. What follows is what I came up with, and what comes closest to my notion of the experience of being in love. When I showed it to someone else, he told me that I couldn't possibly write a book of poems about love without including this:

Putting this feeling into words is just about impossible. Words do communicate to others how we feel, but when it comes to love and passion, words are inadequate, so we look to things like touch and longing gazes to convey what we feel inside. And even that is inadequate. These shells that we call our bodies become our prisons. We cannot fully release that emotion and passion that lies within us when we are with that person who ignites us.

It is like a deep burning ache, in the pit of your gut, that only becomes stronger and more insistent when you are with that person. Here's the difference: When you are not with that person, it seems to be confined to your gut, your core. But when you are together, it is diffused throughout your whole body so that every nerve ending in every part of your body comes alive and sings out with joy and resonates with the other person's. You feel as if your soul is about to burst forth. You shine from within. It's quite nearly an out-of-body experience. It simply transcends the physical and time stands still.

You do not have to say "I love you." This person knows it by your touch, your eyes, your smell, and does not need to hear it, because it can be felt.

Your skin touches and you are no longer two bodies. It's as simple, yet as complex as that.

This is the person who you can talk to for hours and never get bored. This is the person who will never, ever judge you. This is the person who is your soulmate. This is the person whom you should never let go. And when two people are connected at the heart, it does not matter where you go, what you do, or how much distance there is between you.

I truly believe that this kind of love comes only once in a lifetime. It's a cliché, I know, but once you have felt what it's like, you just somehow know that no one else can make you feel quite this way. And once you find that person, you will understand why it never worked out with anyone else before. But life is cruel sometimes, and the truth of the matter is that one day, whether you're 14, 28, or 65, you stumble upon a person who will start a fire in you that cannot die. However, the saddest, most awful truth you will ever come to find is that they are not always the one with whom you spend the rest of your life.

You say the words "love" and "passion" so much and they are so commonplace, but most people utter them without knowing how being with that once-in-a-lifetime person really feels. There's a difference between whom you long for, whom you settle for and whom you are meant for. Unless it's mad, passionate, take-your-breath-away love, it's a waste of time. Life is full of mediocre things. Love should not be one of them.

About the Author

Jill Lapin-Zell is a former English teacher who resides in New Jersey. She has a BA in English from Temple University, an EdM in secondary education from Rutgers University and a Masters in Educational Administration from Rider University.

Some of her poetry has previously appeared in *A Hudson View Poetry Digest*, published by Skyline Publications. She has also edited and written numerous reviews of poetry collections. *Vanishing Into Life* is her first collection of poetry.

www.ingramcontent.com/pod-product-compliance
Lightning Source LLC
LaVergne TN
LVHW021541080426
835509LV00019B/2761